# LEAN INTO YOUR

## 7 STEPS TO MASTERING NONFICTION BOOK STRUCTURE

ALEXANDRA O'CONNELL

*Lean Into Your Yuck: 7 Steps to Mastering Nonfiction Book Structure*
Published by Catamount Publishing
Denver, CO



ISBN: 978-1-7350621-0-5

Self Help / Reference

Cover and Interior design by Victoria Wolf, Wolf Design & Marketing

QUANTITY PURCHASES: Schools, companies, professional groups, clubs, and other organizations may qualify for special terms when ordering quantities of this title. For information, email info@alexoconnell.com.

Printed in the United States of America.

*for Mom & Dad,*
*the believers*

# CONTENTS

# INTRODUCTION

**When I first begin coaching a writer**, our primary goal is to develop a basic structure for their book. Whether or not you are a great believer in outlines, you will, eventually, need structure.

Some people call any structure an outline. I prefer to use the term "Map." **You need an idea of how you're going to get to your destination, but there's nothing worse than feeling like you have to make everything perfect before you start**. Maps are wonderful, flexible tools that you can adapt to your needs: where you are now, where you hope to go, and how to account for any diversions along the way. Outlines, on the other hand, make many people think of school homework and rules that must not be broken.

While you can definitely get somewhere without a map, it may or may not be where you wanted to go, and the trip could take you a long time. Don't be one of those authors with a manuscript languishing in a desk drawer or on some old hard drive for decades.

*Lean Into Your Yuck* is designed to take you through the first part of the process I go through with each of my clients. This particular workbook focuses on nonfiction. That said, if you write fiction or memoir, you can certainly benefit from the suggestions in this workbook!

I've designed this process to be as big picture as possible. Individual books all differ, as do the writers of those books, your thought processes and ideas. Specific details and nuances of your Map will, therefore, also differ from someone else's. However, the landmarks are the same.

The process is simple ... which is not the same as easy. As I tell my coaching clients, **every good coach is there to help you, but they will not do the work *for* you**. YOU need to do the work. In talking about structure, it's important to realize that a lot of the work is thinking, rather than doing. This can be frustrating for people who just want to get to the finish line or complete the exercises (like me!). But thinking is unavoidable and, indeed, the best friend you will have during this process. Take the time to focus and think through your answers.

### How to Use This Workbook

You can go through *Lean Into Your Yuck* as often as you need. In fact, **I recommend you go through it more than once!** As you give yourself time to turn your ideas over in your mind, you'll begin to make new connections and see new possibilities. I recommend you add pages or sticky notes as needed and not delete your previous answers. The record of how your thoughts have evolved can be immensely helpful.

**Revisit your structure throughout the writing process to gauge whether you are on track or not.** In fact, the planners among you can add this to your writing schedule! (See "Step 6.") Writing evolves; you might find your book going in an unexpected direction once you actually begin to write. This is neither good nor bad. Look over your structure, and see where you've diverged from the Map. Is the divergence a valuable addition? Is it a useful new direction? If so, revise your Map. Does the divergent material have you going down a rabbit hole that doesn't have anything useful to do with your book? If so, abandon that rabbit hole and course-correct to your Map.

**You don't need to complete this workbook within a specified timeframe.** On the other hand, it is useful to not draw out the process too much, so that you remember your thoughts and ideas.

When I first meet with a new coaching client, we sit down for two hours. This doesn't mean the Map is complete; I do expect authors to continue working on their own afterwards. You may find one or more intensive sessions work well for you. Or you may find you want to break up the Steps across multiple shorter sessions, giving yourself time to think in between. I will say that because of the way the Steps reference each other, I recommend giving yourself at least an hour at a time.

**What This Workbook Covers**

As Lewis Carroll of *Alice in Wonderland* put it, "Begin at the beginning." First, you'll need an Overview: the WHAT, WHO, and WHYs of your book.

Next, you'll think about your book in the world—aka, in the marketplace as well as the literary environment of ideas. Comparisons provide great information. Don't be a special snowflake ... at least, not yet. Together, Steps 1 and 2 give you your basic structure. In Step 3, you'll practice writing your back blurb ... the first of several times.

After you've had a go at the blurb (don't despair if you found it difficult; you'll have more chances to work with this), in Step 4 we will flesh out your Overview and begin to assemble your Map: the Setup, Body, and Wrap, including details specific to your book.

In Step 5, you'll revisit your blurb, and in Step 6, you'll create a writing schedule, select an accountability buddy (this has to be a willing partner!), and develop a weekly plan.

Boom! We have all the pieces in place ... now it's up to you to use them. Before I set you off on your journey, I close with important notes on how to use your Map so you can receive the most benefit. This includes a discussion of word count goals and a few writing best practices.

After that, "all" you have left is to do the work. As I said, simple—not necessarily easy.

### Use It

Your Map is a living document. I don't want you to feel this is chiseled in stone, then live in fear of ever changing it. We also don't want to forget about the Map. **If you put your Map into a drawer after you've completed it, you're missing the point.** Keep it handy as you write, and refer to it often. I personally feel the Map is best used when it is well-loved: covered in notes and crossed-out text with sticky notes, highlights, and different colored ink for good measure. Your Map isn't a precious object—*the ideas contained in it* are precious. If in the weeks and months after you complete your Map the document remains pristine, this is a red flag.

**What I've provided for you here are analog, rather than digital, tools.** This is by design. When you must use your body to write with a pen and paper, you actually embody the thoughts and ideas of your book and remember and develop them in a deeper way. You internalize concepts. When I meet with clients in person to work on their structure, I can actually watch this happen in real time: their eyes focus and their entire posture changes. We draw all over giant whiteboards, and I can see them putting the puzzle pieces together in their minds. The physical part of this process is powerful.

That said, you may choose to adapt any digital tools you prefer to use. My one recommendation remains that you leave yourself a record of where your thoughts have been along the way—there is no reason to permanently delete anything until well after your book is published. If your Map remains unchanged and unannotated, again, red flag.

Finally, I call this work *leaning into your yuck* for a reason. Yes, this workbook might end up looking messy, but what I mean is the mental "yuck" that all writing seems to involve. **At some stage, often more than once, every writer judges their writing or their ideas as ugly, useless, worthless...as yuck**. Lean into it. Nobody writes a perfect draft out of the gate. The only way out is through.

Only you can do the work. With a good Map in hand, I have faith you'll get to your destination. Bon voyage!

# STEP 1
# OVERVIEW

**You need the following** basic information in order to write a book:

- **WHAT** is it about?
- **WHO** is it for?
- **WHY** do they care? (What's in it for them?)
- **WHY** are you writing the book?

These questions are deceptively simple. Some might be (or appear to be) immediately obvious to you; others will require some thought. Let's go through them one by one.

Remember, what we are putting together is our Map ... we're not making the whole journey. Answer the questions briefly. Bullet points and phrases are the best, a sentence or two at the most. If you find yourself developing an idea further than this, you're already writing.

## WHAT Is Your Book About?

Ah, this seems like the simplest question to answer, but don't be fooled. Plenty of writers start out believing their book is about one thing and discover there's a bigger question they are asking or answering.

## TOPIC

*What is your topic or theme? What is the most important point you are trying to make?*

*In order to develop your topic or theme, what points must you make and what information do you need to share?*

*What genre are you writing?* Carmen Maria Machado describes genre as "a mix of expectation and rules." See alexoconnell.com/know-your-genre for more details on genre.

*Biography*
*Essay*
*Memoir*
*Narrative/Personal*
*Reference*
*Self-Help*
*Speech*
*Textbook*

**CHARACTERS**

*Who are the people in your book?* (Hint: you may be one of the characters.)

*What are their particular struggles, challenges, or problems?*

*What are their special gifts? Their special ideas?*

*What problems or challenges do they solve?*

## RESEARCH

*Do you need to do any research? What information do you need to find that you don't already have?* List your questions here.

*Do you need to interview anyone for more information?* List your potential interviewees here.

________________________________________________

________________________________________________

________________________________________________

________________________________________________

**WHO is Your Book For?**

"Everyone" is not an answer. A (small) group of people is better; one specific person is best.

*Who is reading your book?*

________________________________________________

________________________________________________

________________________________________________

________________________________________________

*What do readers typically expect out of this genre/type of book?*

_______________

_______________

_______________

_______________

*What's your reader's background?* E.g., age, profession, education, language, place they live, etc.

_______________

_______________

_______________

_______________

_______________

_______________

_______________

*What other books do they like to read?*

*What about those books, especially, appeals to them?*

*Do they have a lot of time to read?*

______________________________________________

______________________________________________

______________________________________________

______________________________________________

______________________________________________

______________________________________________

**WHY Do They Care?**
**(What's in it for them?)**

When you begin writing your book, it's quite easy to get caught up in all your good ideas. Remember, you are writing this book for someone else. Writers often get so involved in their own narrative/message they neglect to think about why someone else is reading it. This reason may be similar to, but not the same as, why you're writing. (That's the next question.)

*What is your reader's pain point—how would they describe their pain (their words, not yours)? What does your reader want or need?* (Hint: sometimes they don't know what they want or need until you articulate it.)

___

___

___

___

___

*What problem does your book solve for them?*

___

___

___

___

*What results does your reader get from reading your book?*

*When they recommend your book to their friends, what do they say?*

## WHY Are You Writing This Book?

This question is a two-parter. The first part involves the information you wish to share; the second what you hope to get out of publishing.

**PART 1:**

*What do you want your reader to do, say, or remember as a result of reading your book?*

____________________________________________

____________________________________________

____________________________________________

____________________________________________

*The information in your book is important, valuable, and/or necessary because:*

____________________________________________

____________________________________________

____________________________________________

____________________________________________

**PART 2:**

*What does "success" mean for your book?* Is it strictly what your reader does, says, or remembers, or does it also include:

- Sales target (specific number of books sold)
- Speaking career
- Business builder
- Lead magnet
- Showcase of your expertise
- Other:

______________________________________________

______________________________________________

______________________________________________

**Congratulations! This is your Overview.**

It may change as you continue going through this workbook.
Do not be discouraged; that's the nature of the beast.
We hone our thoughts and ideas over time.

**NEXT: YOUR BOOK IN THE WORLD.**

# STEP 2

# YOUR BOOK IN THE WORLD

**Your book will not live in a void**. The marketplace is full of other books, including books similar to yours. If you don't already know what those similar books are, now is the time to discover them. Traditional publishers call these "comps," short for competitive or comparative titles (see alexoconnell.com/compare-your-book/ for more on comps). Ideally, you'll have two or three. A good comp should be:

- In your genre
- For your reader's age group
- Published within the last five years
- An award-winner or best seller—in other words, a success

*What genre are you writing in?* You may copy this from Step 1.

______________________________________________

______________________________________________

______________________________________________

______________________________________________

*List the books in this genre you have read and particularly like or want to emulate:*

_______________________________________________

_______________________________________________

_______________________________________________

_______________________________________________

_______________________________________________

*WHY? WHAT do you particularly like about these books?*

_______________________________________________

_______________________________________________

_______________________________________________

_______________________________________________

_______________________________________________

*List the books in this genre, if any, you have read and want to avoid being like at all costs. Why do you think these books did poorly?*

________________________________________

________________________________________

________________________________________

________________________________________

*Which authors in your genre do you particularly admire? Why?*

________________________________________

________________________________________

________________________________________

________________________________________

**These are all clues that will help you with "Step 4: Structure!" Before we get there, let's pull these early steps together in the first version of your blurb.**

# STEP 3

# BACK BLURB, ROUND ONE

**The back of the book blurb** is what you find on the back cover or inside flap of a book, describing (or teasing you about) the narrative/message inside. You will have plenty of opportunities to revise and perfect your blurb—we're going to look at it again in this workbook, for one—but for now, our primary goal is a *focus.*

Composing a back blurb before you start writing your book (or if you are stuck in the middle of your process) is a fantastic way to focus your ideas.

The blurb is sales and marketing real estate. An effective blurb distills WHAT the book is about, WHO for, WHY they want to read this book, and WHAT you will give them. *This is not you telling the full narrative* ... that's for inside the covers. Keep it short and sweet.

Ideally, final back cover copy should be no more than 150 words. When you first write your blurb, however, you're most likely describing your book to yourself, and that limit can be difficult to meet. For the purposes of this exercise, try to keep your word count to 250 words or less.

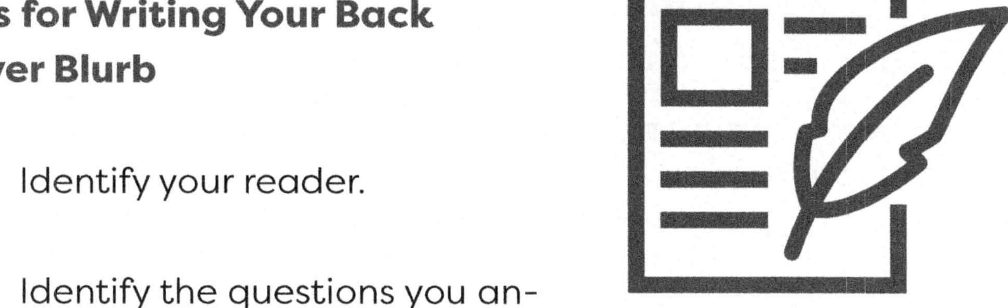

## Tips for Writing Your Back Cover Blurb

- Identify your reader.
- Identify the questions you answer or the problems you solve for your reader.
- Write in the third person and in the active voice.
- Bullet points, short paragraphs, and bolded text are great.
- Are you giving your reader a reason to open the book?
- Optional: Include a minibio of yourself, one or two sentences max. What makes you an expert on this topic? You'll have space for a full bio inside the book.
- The last sentence wraps it up!

# STEP 4
# STRUCTURE!

**At last, we come to** what you've been waiting for. Now that we've addressed the Overview, considered where your book will fit in the wider literary culture and marketplace, and made the first draft of your back cover blurb, let's begin to create your Map.

There are many ways to structure a book. If you go to your local library's database, or to Amazon.com, you can find dozens of approaches. Our goal here is to simplify. I want you to develop the most *basic* landmarks you will use to write your book. You can customize everything you need from here.

The three big pieces of your book are:

- The Setup
- The Body
- The Wrap/Conclusion

Within each of these blocks you may have one or more chapters. **Unless and until you are clear about which ideas are chapter-level (more on this under "The Body" below), don't worry about where your chapter breaks are at this stage.**

Although they appear in this order in your book: Setup > Body > Wrap, you won't necessarily write them in this order. Most often, I recommend creating both the structure (your Map) and the book (when you actually begin writing) in this order: Body > Wrap > Setup.

That being said, you need to begin somewhere. If that means sketching the Setup first, by all means, do so. However, if you find yourself stuck, move on to the Body and do that first.

Let's look at each of these blocks more closely. I'll discuss them in the order we're used to seeing them in a book, for ease.

**The Setup**

The Setup is what it sounds like: You are setting the stage for the rest of your book. This may include pieces such as a Preface and/or an Introduction, if you choose to write them. Chapter 1 may be part of your Setup. As I mention above, the actual chapter breaks are not significant for the purposes of creating your initial Map.

Because the Setup and the Wrap are so closely related, you will most likely finalize your Setup after you've written the Wrap.

The Setup *must* include:

- A **hook** to grab your reader (WHO)
- An introduction to your major **topic or theme** (WHAT)
- An introduction to **you as the author** (WHY you are writing the book, including any relevant expertise you have)
- WHY the ***reader* cares** about your book
- What you want them to **do, feel, or remember** (your WHY)

The Setup may also include a rundown of the major supporting points the Body covers and in what order.

### Hook, Line, and Sinker

**The Setup takes up a relatively small percentage of your book's total word count, but these words determine whether your reader decides to go any further or not.** You need to immediately grab their attention and give them reasons to invest their time (and money!) in your book. This is what we mean by "hook." You want to hook your reader's interest, and by that, I mean from Page 1, from the very first sentence, if possible. No warm-up, no long lead-in, no backstory. Immediately.

A good hook necessarily takes into account your reader's interests, pain points, background, beliefs, preferences, expectations, and more. You had better care about your reader, because that's the only way you'll get them to care about your book.

Sound hard yet? This is typically the part of writing a book that authors struggle with most and also the reason that I advocate writing the Setup last. I do, however, highly recommend you do the preparatory work in Steps 1 through 3 of this workbook before you begin *any* writing because if you have no ideas about your audience, no amount of words in the Body will help you write your Setup.

Remember, in all cases, the Setup involves *introducing* ideas. If you find yourself *developing* them, you've moved into the Body.

## YOUR BOOK: SETUP

**PART 1:**
Review your answers to Steps 1 through 3. Write this information again here for your Setup.

*What is your major topic or theme?*

*Do you have any expertise in this subject? Why are you writing the book?*

*Why does your reader care about your book?*

*What will they do, feel, or remember after they read?*

*What, if any of this, could become part of your hook?* Highlight, underline, or circle key words/phrases.

Write the first draft of your hook here:

______________________________________________

______________________________________________

______________________________________________

______________________________________________

______________________________________________

______________________________________________

**PART 2:**

**Once you've created the structure for the Body**, go back and look at your Setup again. Does the Setup include information that doesn't appear in the Body? Make sure to add any new pieces to the Body portion of your Map.

**PART 3:**

**Once you've created the structure for your Wrap,** look at your Setup again. Do the Setup and Wrap mirror each other? If not, does one or both need adjusting? The material you introduce in the Setup should reach some form of closure in the Wrap; material you highlight in the Wrap needs to be introduced in the Setup. Revise the Setup as needed.

Additional NOTES or space to (re)write your Setup/Hook

## The Body

The Body makes up the bulk of your book's word count. All of the details and supporting arguments of your book must appear here. The Body fleshes out your overall topic and theme, and addresses your audience's WHY.

You may choose to begin creating your Map with this step, or with the Setup.

Start with the ideas you wrote down in "Step 1: Overview."

*What is your topic or theme? What is the most important point you are trying to make?* Rewrite this here:

______________________________________________

______________________________________________

______________________________________________

______________________________________________

______________________________________________

______________________________________________

______________________________________________

*In order to develop your topic or theme, what points must you make or what information do you need to share?* These are candidates for your chapters. Rewrite them here:

Are any of your supporting points or information chapter-sized? Place a check mark next to these or highlight them. To clarify what "chapter-sized" means, ask yourself:

- What does my reader expect? Are they looking for in-depth discussions? Do they accept a higher or lower density of content? How clear and succinct do they want me to be? Scale your chapter prototypes to audience needs.

- Are any of your supporting points supportive of *each other*, or do they support the main topic or theme *directly*? Only those that support the main topic or theme directly are chapter-sized. Other material can be incorporated within chapters.

- If you are unsure of the chapter breaks, you can begin by treating the supporting points separately as smaller sections and come back to them once you've written the material. Once you've started writing, you usually begin to see where the chapter breaks are. If this is the case for you, cluster your material as above.

Space for your baby Map is given below. Write down your chapter prototypes/sections. Underneath each chapter prototype or section heading, add:

- The supporting point or information you discuss in that chapter

- One specific example (at minimum) from your experience or research that illustrates the supporting point. You may add more than one ... though be careful of an overabundance of examples in a single chapter

- Why this chapter exists (This note is for yourself, and will be helpful in creating chapter Conclusions as well as the book Wrap.)

Do you need to do any research or conduct any interviews to glean the information you need to write this section? Make a note of these questions in the appropriate chapter(s).

Tips for when you actually begin writing the Body:

- Use specific sensory detail where possible: what things look like, sound like, smell like, feel like, etc. For example, say, "The drops from my water bottle sizzled on the pavement," rather than, "It was hot."

- Remember, for the reader, this book is about *their* problems. Gear what you write to them, not yourself. What questions do they have?

- Why is what you want to discuss important?

## YOUR BOOK: BODY

### PART 1: CREATING CHAPTERS AND SECTIONS

Following are ten sets of five questions so you can create your first ten chapters/sections.

**Possible chapter or section prototype #1:**

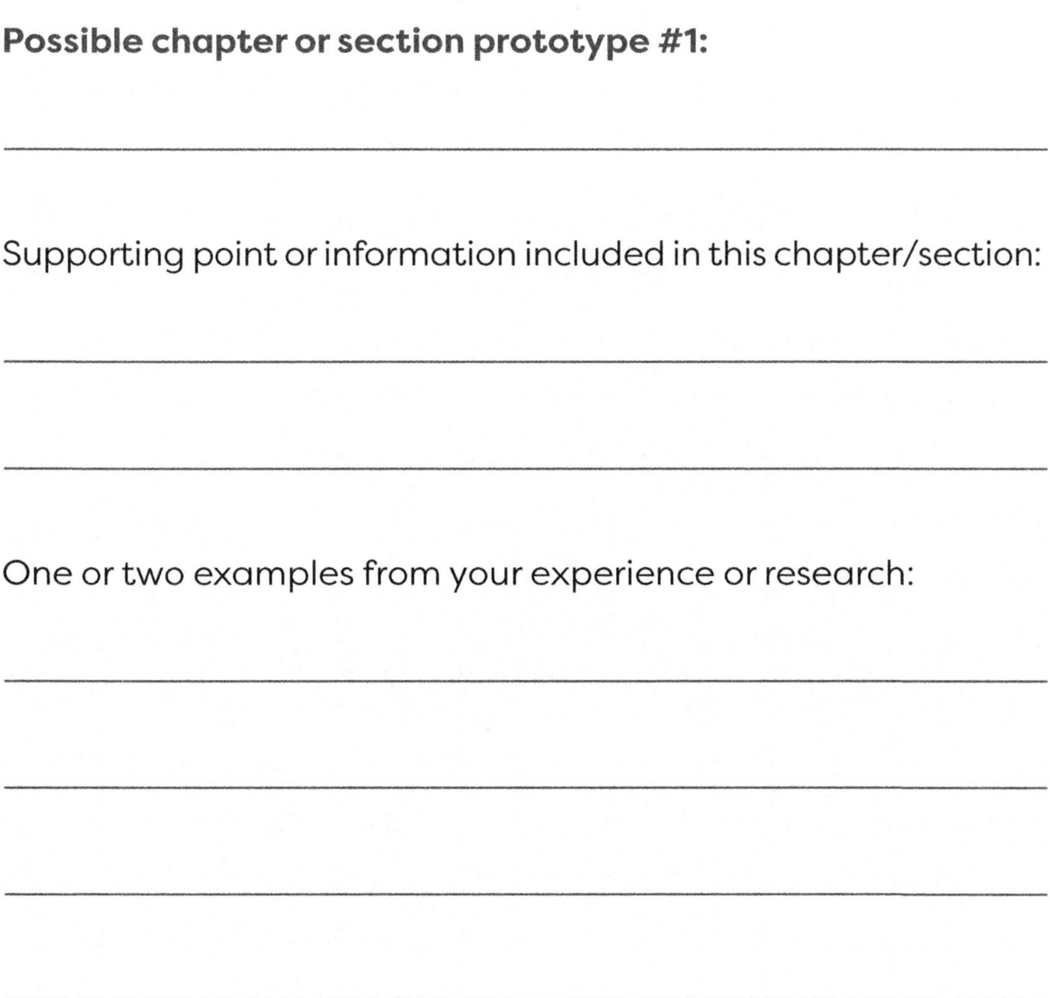

Supporting point or information included in this chapter/section:

One or two examples from your experience or research:

Why you need this chapter/section:

_______________________________________________

_______________________________________________

Research you need for this chapter/section:

_______________________________________________

_______________________________________________

_______________________________________________

_______________________________________________

_______________________________________________

_______________________________________________

**Possible chapter or section prototype #2:**

_______________________________________________

Supporting point or information included in this chapter/section:

---

---

One or two examples from your experience or research:

---

---

---

---

Why you need this chapter/section:

---

---

Research you need for this chapter/section:

---

---

**Possible chapter or section prototype #3:**

Supporting point or information included in this chapter/section:

One or two examples from your experience or research:

Why you need this chapter/section:

________________________________________

________________________________________

Research you need for this chapter/section:

________________________________________

________________________________________

________________________________________

________________________________________

________________________________________

________________________________________

**Possible chapter or section prototype #4:**

______________________________________________

Supporting point or information included in this chapter/section:

______________________________________________

______________________________________________

One or two examples from your experience or research:

______________________________________________

______________________________________________

______________________________________________

______________________________________________

Why you need this chapter/section:

______________________________________________

______________________________________________

Research you need for this chapter/section:

**Possible chapter or section prototype #5:**

Supporting point or information included in this chapter/section:

One or two examples from your experience or research:

Why you need this chapter/section:

Research you need for this chapter/section:

**Possible chapter or section prototype #6:**

---

Supporting point or information included in this chapter/section:

---

---

One or two examples from your experience or research:

---

---

---

---

Why you need this chapter/section:

---

---

Research you need for this chapter/section:

**Possible chapter or section prototype #7:**

Supporting point or information included in this chapter/section:

One or two examples from your experience or research:

Why you need this chapter/section:

Research you need for this chapter/section:

**Possible chapter or section prototype #8:**

Supporting point or information included in this chapter/section:

One or two examples from your experience or research:

Why you need this chapter/section:

Research you need for this chapter/section:

**Possible chapter or section prototype #9:**

Supporting point or information included in this chapter/section:

One or two examples from your experience or research:

Why you need this chapter/section:

Research you need for this chapter/section:

**Possible chapter or section prototype #10:**

______________________________________________

Supporting point or information included in this chapter/section:

______________________________________________

______________________________________________

One or two examples from your experience or research:

______________________________________________

______________________________________________

______________________________________________

______________________________________________

Why you need this chapter/section:

______________________________________________

______________________________________________

Research you need for this chapter/section:

______________________________________________

______________________________________________

______________________________________________

______________________________________________

______________________________________________

______________________________________________

**PART 2:**

Go back to your Setup. (A) Does the Setup include information that doesn't appear in the Body? Adjust as necessary. (B) Does the Body include information that needs to be introduced in the Setup? Adjust as necessary.

Additional NOTES

______________________________________________

______________________________________________

______________________________________________

## The Wrap

Think of the Wrap and the Setup as two sides of the same coin—they share the same backbone. In practical terms, the content in one echoes the other. It is often much easier to write the Wrap before the Setup. Your Wrap must:

- Provide some form of closure for your main topic or theme. An emotional close is often better than an intellectual one (again, consider your genre), though you can have both

- Tie together, reiterate, or somehow rephrase the message from the Body of the book

- Remember the reader's WHY

The Wrap may include some kind of call to action if you like: what you want the reader to do, say, or remember.

The Wrap must *not*:

- Add new material. New material should appear in the Body first.

Percentagewise, the Wrap is much smaller than the Body. **You may need very little to deliver closure.** Your Wrap may consist of a final chapter, or even only paragraph or two. Some books use a Conclusion section. Name it whatever works for you.

Look at the chapter prototype headings. Do you want to address them individually in the Wrap, or can you treat them as a group? Make a note to yourself under "Wrap" below.

Do you find yourself wanting to add new material to the Wrap? Revisit the Body, and add that material where appropriate, first.

What do you want your reader to do, say, or remember? Add this to "Your Book: Wrap" below. Also, add any call to action you might have.

The Wrap is incredibly important. This is what you're leaving your reader with, your final opportunity to address them and their needs. Just as with the Setup, think about your reader and what they want and need!

## YOUR BOOK: WRAP

**PART 1:**

*Wrap chapters together or individually?*

*Is any of this material new?*

*What I want my reader to do/say/remember:*

*Call to action, if any:*

______________________________________________

______________________________________________

______________________________________________

______________________________________________

______________________________________________

**PART 2:**
Go back to your Setup. (A) Does the Setup include information that doesn't appear in the Wrap? Adjust as necessary. (B) Does the Wrap include information that needs to be introduced in the Setup? Adjust as necessary.

Are you beginning to see your book take shape?

Additional NOTES or space to (re)write your Wrap/Conclusion

______________________________________________

______________________________________________

______________________________________________

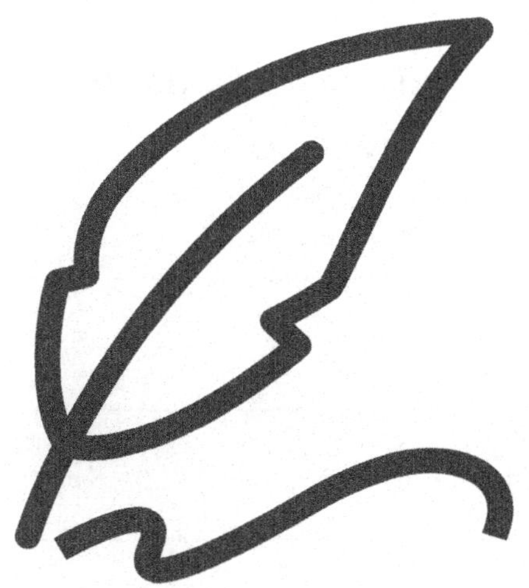

# STEP 5

# BACK BLURB, REVISITED

**It's been a while since** we looked at the blurb. Let's visit this again. Your first draft of the back blurb was a focusing exercise. This time, we use the back blurb to check if you're still on track.

Take a look at your blurb draft. *Does this line up with your Wrap and your Setup? Why or why not?*

*Do you want to make adjustments to your blurb?* Draft another version here:

Do you want to make adjustments to your Wrap? Keep in mind, adjustments to the Wrap > adjustments to the Setup > possibly revision of the Body. Once you make the changes in one, follow the thread all the way through.

# STEP 6
# CREATE A WRITING SCHEDULE

**You're almost done!** Your baby Map now includes the three major pieces of any book: the Setup, Body, and Wrap (or Conclusion). You've focused on your audience and why you are writing this book, and you've thought about where the book fits in the wider publishing and literary ecosystem. The final step before you begin writing is to create your writing schedule.

As I tell my clients, everyone has an idea. **Books are about ideas plus focus over a long period of time.** The main barrier to completing a book is making a habit of sitting down to write it.

The more you stay in touch with your book by working on it regularly, the easier the process of writing becomes. Once every two weeks is not going to cut it. An hour a week isn't going to get you far, either. What I'm asking you to do is to commit to a schedule up front, and block out this time.

Some people prefer to work on their manuscript daily; others prefer to block out larger chunks of time on fewer days during the week, such as all day Thursday, or Wednesday and Friday mornings. As long as you are dedicating at least five hours of time to your book each week, I am happy with whatever schedule works best for you.

Let's get down to it.

## Schedule

*What day(s) each week will you write?*

______________________________________________________________

______________________________________________________________

*What time(s)?*

______________________________________________________________

______________________________________________________________

## Weekly Plan

Now that you have your basic schedule, add specific details below. You may write your notes here, or modify them on a separate sheet of paper or file. Make sure the schedule and your weekly plan are visible from the place where you sit down to write. You may wish to tape this to your computer or the wall behind it.

At the start of each week, set yourself a weekly schedule. What chapter(s) will you work on this week?

Week 1: [Date]____________________

[Content]______________________________________________________

Week 2: [Date]________________

[Content]____________________________________________

Week 3: [Date]________________

[Content]____________________________________________

Week 4: [Date]________________

[Content]____________________________________________

Week 5: [Date]________________

[Content]____________________________________________

Week 6: [Date]________________

[Content]____________________________________________

Week 7: [Date]________________

[Content]____________________________________________

Week 8: [Date]________________

[Content]____________________________________________

Week 9: [Date]________________

[Content]____________________________________________

... and so on. You don't need to plan too far ahead—you can address the content you want to write week by week. If you feel extra "plan-y" you may add a time to revisit "Step 4: Structure!" at certain intervals.

I like checking things off lists and marking digital reminders "complete." You can use these same tools yourself to track your accomplishments. Make sure your accountability buddy knows your plans and will hold your feet to the fire (see below).

**Two Notes on Research**

(1) Research (including interviews) should go on your schedule, just as the writing does. You can use your writing schedule to do research as long as you set yourself specific goals (aka, you need specific questions answered). Revisit the Overview for those questions, and add any more that you need.

(2) Research is best if you do it separate from your writing (i.e., your writing day will ideally be spent on *either* research, *or* writing).

**Accountability Buddy**

Goals are much easier to achieve when someone is holding you accountable. Who is your accountability buddy? This should be someone willing! Don't "appoint" them without letting them know.

______________________________________________

*Will they check in with you, or you with them?*

______________________________________________

*When/how often?*

______________________________________________

Make sure your accountability buddy knows your weekly plan(s)! Now, take your writing schedule, and post it where you can see it every day from your desk or wherever you write your book.

# IMPLEMENTING THE PLAN

## Implementing the Plan

You have now created a starter Map to write your book. Congratulations! The next step is sitting down to do the actual writing. Before we go there, though, **I want to remind you of how to use your Map, and how NOT to use it.**

Your writing schedule means you have set aside time to write or research on a regular basis. **How you DO want to use your writing schedule**: look at your Structure first and decide what details to pursue.

**How you DO NOT want to use your writing schedule**: diving in blindly without checking the Map.

## Word Count

You may find that the use of word count goals helps you to keep to your schedule and gives you a sense of completion. The beauty of word count goals is how objective and measurable they are. You immediately know whether you've achieved them. If you write 500 words per day, five days per week, you will have 2,500 words per week and 10,000 per month. Awesome!

The potential disadvantage of a word count goal is if you feel the pressure to hit the word count without taking your Map/Structure into account. Let me say this loud and clear: **all word count goals should be in service of your Structure.** I have worked with too many people who started a book with a great idea and in the process of writing, have disappeared down rabbit holes-turned-interstellar vortices. Not so awesome.

**How to use word count goals:**

- Create a *minimum* goal. If you blow past it—great! Note that it'll be easier to blow past your minimum while writing the Body and harder when you get to the Setup and the Wrap.

- Every session is a fresh start. Word counts do not carry over. If you have set yourself a 500 words/day goal and you write 800 words today, that doesn't let you off the hook for at least 500 tomorrow. If you write 4,000 words this week, that doesn't let you off the hook for 2,500 next week, and so on.

- If you find yourself regularly blowing past your minimum, consider raising the minimum a modest amount.

- Don't let the vortices get you. If you find the word counts create a weird pressure on your writing, toss them out. I'd much rather you keep your writing schedule (Step 6).

## Other Tips for Staying on the Map

1. When you begin writing, **start with the low-hanging fruit.** By this, I mean start with whatever seems easiest to you at the time. You want to accumulate words, not sit there stuck. Eventually, you will get to the hard stuff, and it may or may not still be "hard" at that point.

2. **You do not need to write the content in any particular order.** Your reader will never know!

3. **Writing is separate from research.** If, while writing, you have questions for more research, make a note of these under Research in the Body of your Structure, and carry on writing. Later, schedule research time. What you want to avoid is disappearing into the bowels of the internet/source material instead of working on your book. Remember, you have a separate space on your schedule for this!

4. **Writing is separate from editing.** My number one goal for you right now is to complete a first draft. I have met writers who spend years on incomplete manuscripts because they can't stop rewriting earlier chapters. Take a look at your Map—have you hit the main points? Good. Don't worry about the poetry of how you've written it UNTIL YOU HAVE FINISHED THE WHOLE MANUSCRIPT.

5. As much as possible, **forward motion**. This is a corollary to number 4. Don't reread your chapter until you've completed a full draft of it. Is this the third time you've rewritten Chapter 3? Red flag! Time to move on ... or to check in with your Map (see ***** below).

6. **Leave a "jagged edge" at the end of your writing session**—stop in the middle of an idea, topic, story, or even sentence. It'll make it easier when you start again.

*****The most important tip is to **check in with your Map on a regular basis.** Your Map may evolve as you write. This is normal. If this happens, what I want you to ask yourself is: "Am I writing a completely different book than the Map I've put together?"

If no, and there are only minor course corrections—great! Make sure you incorporate these into your Map.

If yes, revisit your Overview. Is this still the book you want to write? If it is—great! You've caught yourself going down a rabbit hole-possibly-interstellar vortex. Time to course-correct what you are writing.

If the Overview isn't the book you want to write anymore but your current deviation is—also great. You've uncovered really important information. Time to create a new Map!

**Your Road Map is a Tool, Not a Rule**

Remember, in "How to Use This Workbook" I suggested you can go through these steps as often as you need to. The point is to create a structure that works for you, and the fact is, you'll continue to discover ways your book works throughout the process of creating your Map, through writing and beyond. If you find you need to make a change—do it! Nobody is grading you on how much you adhered to the first draft of your plan. Pit stops are great during road trips and while writing.

# STEP 7

# STARTING THE JOURNEY

**As a certain ad tells us** ... "Go forth and do that thing!" (Well, you know what I mean.)

You now have a baby Map. It's time to take a seat behind the wheel. Parting tips:

- Celebrate and reward yourself when you've achieved a milestone. Our brains love dopamine!
- If you need a helping hand, let me know. I am happy to support you. We can set up a brainstorming session or consultation anytime. Sometimes writers need to get out of their own heads.
- Books are about ideas plus focus over a long period of time. The main barrier to completing a book is making the habit of sitting down to write it.

Lean into your yuck. I believe in you. You can do this. Happy writing!

# ACKNOWLEDGMENTS

**Anyone who has ever written a book** knows that the final product is a team effort. That is true for all books, including short workbooks like this!

With gratitude for the folks who have had a hand in this book particularly: Cathy Spader, Sara Rosinsky, and Joyce Feustel for editorial feedback; Jen Zelinger for proofing with sass; Victoria Wolf for somehow translating my thoughts (and hand-waving while on the phone) into gorgeous layout and design; and Polly Letofsky for all the project know-how, enthusiasm, and generally keeping it real. You are all amazing. Thanks also to all my editorial colleagues over the years for sharing ideas, support, and good humor and for showcasing absolute professionalism always.

With gratitude for my many friends, personal and professional, who have helped me refine my ideas; all the authors who have entrusted their work to my care; and the Colorado Independent Publishers Association for providing a platform and guidance for independent authors everywhere. You are my community. This wouldn't be here without you!

And last but not least, for all of my family—the great O'Tribe, wherever you are in the world—your love and support in all things sustains me always. I love you.

# ABOUT THE AUTHOR

**Alexandra is an award-winning** editor, writer, and writing coach in Denver, Colorado. She received second place for editing in the 2019 CIPA EVVY Awards, for *The Modern Compassionate Leader* by James Michael Martin, and first and second place for editing in the 2018 CIPA EVVY Awards for *To the Sound of the Guns* by Grady Birdsong and *Adventures with Durango Pete* by Stephen Hinman, respectively. Her authors' books have won numerous individual awards—at the CIPA EVVYs and elsewhere—as well (for which she'd like to accept *some* credit). She has helped authors publish memoirs, fiction, and books on business and leadership, health, spirituality, and more. On launch day, she is notoriously as excited as the authors themselves.

Alexandra is the past president and former marketing chair of the Colorado Independent Publishers Association, a nonprofit, statewide cooperative of authors, independent book publishers, and publishing professionals. She earned her M.Phil. in applied linguistics from Trinity College, Dublin and her B.A. in European studies from The College of William and Mary, as well as studying linguistics at the University of Canterbury, New Zealand. When she's not working with words, she's likely to be outside somewhere because other than with literature, that's the best place to be.

**Follow Alexandra on LinkedIn, Twitter, and at www.alexoconnell.com.**

# WHAT'S NEXT?

Writing, of course! And if you've gotten this far, then I've got a gift to help you with exactly that.

Go to **alexoconnell.com/whats-next** to download a free writing schedule template.

The hardest part of writing is often just sticking to the schedule. Give yourself an extra boost and set up a new, effective writing habit by downloading the schedule template today.

You can also find links there to schedule a free, 20-minute consultation, and information on:

- Book Structure Intensive sessions
- Ongoing coaching for your writing
- Manuscript evaluations
- Book editing
- Back cover copy review

Take your first step in writing your book at **alexoconnell.com/whats-next** today!

# ENJOY THIS BOOK? WRITE A REVIEW!

If you've found this workbook helpful, the best compliment you can give is an honest review. It only takes a few minutes, and it helps other readers. Thank you!

# NOTES

## NOTES

# NOTES

# NOTES

# NOTES

## NOTES

# NOTES

Made in the USA
Las Vegas, NV
07 February 2022